INSUFFICIENT FUNDS

(ONE WOMAN'S JOURNEY OUT OF DEBT AND INTO FINANCIAL FREEDOM)

Lauren Greutman

D0451558

Foreword

My wife is a big thinker and always throws herself headlong into whatever she does. Ideas come and go; the good ones stick, and the bad ones tend to fade. A few months ago, Lauren had another big idea. This time, she wanted to write a book about our story over the past decade– the good, the bad and well, you know the rest. She wanted to include our failures as well as our triumphs and how we overcame some dire financial situations. Her intentions were great – anyone who feels financially over-burdened would relate to our story. But if I'm being honest, I was hoping that this idea of hers would fade.

I could only focus on those dire financial situations. They challenged our marriage and faith; and yes, we have overcome a great deal in a short amount of time. But here's what I couldn't get past – for the most part, these situations weren't the product of mere bad fortune. We created our own circumstances, and we could have avoided them. Like many husbands, I've always had a 'man of the house' attitude towards our family finances, and taken responsibility for all that results. So what did those situations say about me as the leader of my household? Again, my mind could only focus on the negative.

As Lauren will demonstrate, we made some poor financial decisions. I have trouble disclosing these details to friends and coworkers, so the idea of sharing with everyone who reads is a blow to my ego. I scored a 760 on the math SAT, I graduated magna cum laude with a dual major in math and economics, and I am a credentialed actuary. I understand all the mathematical mechanics behind the time value of money. Yet I still made many boneheaded decisions.

But somewhere along the way, I warmed up to this 'book' idea. Lauren always tells me that I need to lighten up in all matters of life, and she's right. As embarrassing as parts of this story might be to me, I suspect I'm not completely alone, especially as a guy. I'm not the only one feeling shame for guiding my family to financial peril; and I'm not alone in the humiliation of not being able to make my monthly household budget balance, let alone save anything towards retirement or college for my children. But just as guys don't like to talk about their feelings, they don't like discussing how financially strapped they might be. And from a woman's perspective, I can only imagine that you may feel absolutely overwhelmed with raising children, feeding your family, doing laundry, kids' homework, etc. all while possibly working a part-time or full-time job. And these tendencies certainly don't encourage dialogue regarding household economics.

My recent change of heart has taught me one more humbling lesson: my 'manly pride' over the years has prevented me from taking true responsibility of my decisions, and made the road to recovery longer than it should have. I'm not afraid anymore. This book contains all of the dirty details, and I'm okay with it. This is a discussion that needs to take place much more often than it does.

The whole point of this book is that it isn't just "our story;" a lot of it might be "your story," too. Over the past few years, Lauren has had the opportunity to speak to many women, and the overriding theme has been difficulty in taking control of finances and debt while trying to juggle the rest of life. It can be done. And no matter what your role is in your family, you can make HUGE contributions. We hit bottom, but we climbed out all while raising a growing family, moving multiple times, and with shifting employment.

I'm glad Lauren wrote this book. It will give you some insight, whether it be to simply laugh at our mistakes (it's okay, we laugh, too), to confirm that you are not alone, or to find hope that there is a way out.

Prologue

It's not uncommon for people to have financial troubles--not in this day and age of easy credit, and the promise of "having it all." Television, the internet and magazines show everyone using iPhones, buying the newest electronics, carrying Coach purses and driving around cars they probably can't afford.

But was this our dream? We were so focused on acquiring all the material things 'we thought' we needed and deserved, that we never stopped to examine our spending, let alone determine where we wanted our money to take us. I realize now that we were so concerned with appearances that we felt ashamed to turn down double dates, vacations, and kids attractions.

My mother's favorite phrase came to mind: "It takes two to tango." Mark and I got into this together. Now we'd work as partners to get out and rebuild our relationship, life, and finances.

I needed to work to help pay the bills, so I got a full time job, but I didn't like being away from my family every night. After realizing we were spending roughly $1,000 per month on food related purchases, we knew we had to cut back drastically. No, we didn't eat lobster every night but we ate like most Americans do. Eat out a few times per week but still spend over $150 at the grocery store, food goes to waste and you have to buy more. It is a cycle that far too many people are in. My challenge to myself was to be able to quit my job and stay home with our son; in order to do this I had to cut that $1,000 in food down to only $200 per month. I would learn how to meal plan and use coupons. That was a start. After learning how to save in this one area of my life, couponing because a catalyst for saving everywhere else in my life. I was less likely to make impulsive purchases when I had just worked so hard to save $50 at the grocery store. I was officially a work at home mom, but my job was to *save* money instead of make money. It pretty much is the same thing if you look at it in an hourly wage.

What follows is our journey from being in approximately $40,000 worth of debt, to becoming debt free. Some mornings I woke up and felt the weight of the debt on my chest; it was so overwhelming and I had no idea how we were going to get out of it. There were a lot of tears, doubt, confusion, and eventually determination to get out of it!

It's not rocket science. And I'm not a CPA or a financial guru. I'm a wife and the mother of four children. I turned my life around with some common sense, discipline, and a lot of hard work. And I'm here to show you that you can do it, too!

I hope my story inspires you to make a heart connection with your money, because when that happens, everything changes for the better.

TEARS, FEARS & TOO MANY CREDIT CARDS

{February 2007}

Fast forward to fall 2007 and you'll find us sitting on the queen bed in our huge master bedroom suite, in the $225,000 custom built home that we should never have bought. It was way over our budget to begin with. The bedroom alone was larger than our first apartment, and it's full of stuff--a TV, couch, and an elliptical trainer, to name a few. Many of these items were purchased with credit cards because we could not afford them. But we felt like we needed to have them to fill up our once empty house.

I was in tears. I felt like a failure as a wife and mom. I was exhausted and broke, not to mention feeling utterly hopeless. Scattered around us on the bed is the undeniable proof of our credit cards that were all maxed out, school loans, car payments, and all our bills. We were 26 years old, over $40,000 in debt, unable to make even the minimum payments on our credit cards, let alone pay for our living expenses. We'd cut back on everything we could, got rid of our home phone, cancelled our cable, cut our food bill down drastically, and we were still losing ground every month to the tune of $1,000. We felt like we were drowning. I began wondering if we'd make it through this; after all, most divorces are a consequence of financial issues. Were we strong enough to make it through this?

Mark was still making a good living to support us, but my once lucrative job in sales had dried up. His paycheck couldn't save us from our downward spiral. He was not making enough to pay our bills and our minimum credit payments. We knew for months that we were in financial crisis, but we'd fooled ourselves into thinking we could rein in our spending. I hid the credit cards statements from Mark because I was embarrassed, and Mark was too afraid to ask me how much debt we were in. Because we weren't talking about it, the debt kept growing. We both knew it was there, but we simply ignored it.

Instead, we played games--paying off one credit card with balance transfers from another, jumping into zero balance credit cards but ignoring the large fees, and the eventual day of double digit interest rates that always came back to haunt us. We'd never taken true stock of our mess. We'd never, *together*, sat down like this to look at the damage we'd done--mutually, recklessly, and with abandon.

Mark was numb.

I was crying.

We were both scared and feeling hopeless.

Mark quietly asked, *"Is this just the way it's going to be the rest of our lives, struggling to get by?"* I was crying because I felt ashamed for hiding the credit cards from Mark, and because I'd spent so much money. I began to wonder how we would have more children if we couldn't afford the one that we had. My heart as a mom and wife was broken. This was not where I thought I'd be at this age.

For the first time we were owning up to the dire consequences of our crazy, no holds-barred spending. And the sight of those cards, the tally of all those bills, was our day of reckoning.

It was terrifying.

Like many in our generation, we started out with grand plans and good intentions. But along the way, we got lost. We allowed ourselves to be swept along on a ride of having it all now and paying for it later. But we never paid for it, and consequently, the total owed was crippling. The weight of debt is all the same; $10,000 to one person will feel the same as $200,000 to another. Being in over $40,000 was the end.of.us.

In our rush to get all the things we wanted, we'd forgotten our core values -- being responsible and building a future for our family. Now I realized I would have to find new employment, probably outside of the home, pulling me further away from what I valued most-- being with my husband and son. I knew I had to work-to get us out of this predicament.

Although technically we'd gotten into this together, I felt more responsible, like it was my spending habits that ultimately led to this mess. Mark felt complicit, but I carried the greater share of guilt. He went along, but I had taken the lead early on in the finances.

Through all these trials and hardships, our marriage remained strong. I feel like this was a miracle. Despite many marriages failing due to money stress, we made it through. There were lots of fights and even more prayers. We had to have constant communication about who was spending what, and with that came confrontation when one had spent too much. Struggling with your money may be hardest part of any marriage. I am so grateful we made it through this very difficult time.

We were still a team, and now we had to funnel all our faith, strength, and love into building a new life, one based on sound financial decisions. We started by putting our heads together to find a way out. We'd remembered some Dave Ramsey Financial Peace University CD's we'd heard about - great ideas, we thought at the time. We told ourselves back then that we didn't have time and it was too hard to implement. Now, it seemed like the only answer. We actually decided to listen to his CD's, read some of his books, and started trying to put his theories into practice.

I put away my tear-soaked Kleenex and went out and got a job. Not the glamorous sales job I'd started with, which fell apart, but a waitressing job in a restaurant. I hadn't worked for someone else in a long time, and when asked my previous employment history I felt foolish, and embarrassed to report that I had failed as a business owner and now needed money to feed my family.It's funny how that fear tried to keep my from getting this job, but I knew that I needed to provide for my family. I am an all or nothing person, and this was the time to be all in to make money to help my husband.

"PRINCESS" MEETS HER PRINCE

{Summer 2001}

I met my husband Mark as a sophomore at a state university in Upstate, New York. I too was from New York, but from Saratoga Springs, a town known for its Thoroughbred racetrack, white pillared houses and upscale boutiques along Main Street, fancy restaurants, resorts, and money. Everywhere I looked, money offered the promise of "the good life," and everything that went along with it.

Mark's smaller hometown was worlds away from the Saratoga bling I saw growing up. It's in New York's proverbial "rust belt," where major businesses have moved away, leaving high unemployment, closed shops on Main Street, and a largely blue collar population. But it's also a place where people know the value of a dollar, love their hometown, and continually work to revive their community.

My state school was my college of choice for three important reasons: the Criminal Justice program was strong, and this was my major; I had been recruited for the field hockey team there; and finally, my parents had gone there, met and fallen in love on that campus. Little did I know what else fate had in store for me in that decision, which turned out to be the best of my life.

The summer between my sophomore and junior years, I decided to stay in my new college town rather than going home. I worked a job bartending, and worked with the college theatre program. I was learning to love this town where highlights included an annual summer festival, a three-day celebration of music and food, where bands played into the night along the shores of Lake Ontario. Life was simpler here than back home, and I enjoyed it. Most of all, I was falling in love with a guy I saw playing drums in my church, a talented guy I'd heard about from his sister who was in the youth group.

While I was nicknamed "The Princess" by my family for my uptown tastes and somewhat lazy ways, Mark was truly a prince--hard-working, academic, attending college on a scholarship in economics and math, and a musician--who loved drums and the rock group "Rush." He valued family, wanted to make his parents proud with his achievements, and saw education as a way to move up in the world and better his life.

Then I came along. It's significant that we met in church, for despite some outward differences of background and geography, our Christian faith was and still is our first priority. It's what brought us together, what binds us and forms the foundation of our lives on a daily basis.

While I came from a town full of money, my family and Mark's were more similar than one might guess. My parents were hard working. My dad was first a school teacher and later was employed by General Electric. He and my mom built our home together from scratch. I grew up with a mother who knew the value of a deal, loved bargain hunting, and taught me the tricks of the trade. Whenever we went shopping, we always checked the clearance racks first, and rarely paid full price for anything. She was, however, quick to pull a credit card from her wallet to pay for those "deals." My father's work ethic, very much like Mark's, and his father's, was engrained in me from my earliest years. It took me a long time to realize that I was smart and a hard worker. It wasn't until I met Mark who challenged me in many ways I never had before, that I realized my full potential in life.

My parents provided all the necessities and more. While I was, as my sisters insisted, a "princess," (I've since lost that title!), I always knew that if I wanted something "over the top" extra, like a designer purse, I had to work for it. From the age of 16, I was bussing tables and working in local shops in town.   I never wanted to go without the things I dreamed about, even from an early age.

Mark came from a family of similar values, but lesser means. His father owned an upholstery business, and his mother, who had a Master's degree in Education, chose to stay home and raise her four children. While Mark never went without, he knew from an early age that if he wanted anything extra-- toys or a bike, he'd have to work and save for it. His family never used credit cards and taught him to live frugally. At the age of nine he had a paper route, and used that money to buy anything extra that he wanted. In high school, he was given $100 a year for clothes. If he wanted anything beyond that, he had to work and pay for it himself. This habit stayed with him in college, where he worked summers for spending money, and bought his first car with cash--a rusty, used Nissan Stanza. It was practically falling apart, but he paid for it with cash – a foreign idea to me at the time. Education was important in his family. He studied hard, earned excellent grades, and received an academic scholarship to college.

He was a saver, I was a spender. He had his dreams too, like driving an Audi, and maybe living in a high-rise apartment in New York City. But he never expected to get those things without hard work and thrift. He lived according to those values growing up and into college. He was on track to make a good life for himself, and had no thoughts of marriage when we met, telling me that he didn't want a wedding until he was 40. He assumed it would take time to build a career and a solid savings account.

And then we started to hang out and

soon after began dating. From the minute I laid eyes on him playing in the band at our church, I found myself falling in love. I had dated enough jocks and jerks in high school to know that this guy was different. Quiet, considerate, studious, serious, and of course handsome!

Mark had no intentions of marrying young. He was going to move on and away from his hometown, follow his career path, and steer toward The Big Apple. But apparently, he was falling in love too, and we became inseparable. That summer in 2001 we knew we were going to get married. We even started making wedding plans, although many discouraged us by saying that we were too young. After the summer we met, I visited him at his college frequently, horrified to find nothing more than frozen pizzas and some Ramen noodles in the cupboard. I spent much of our time on those weekends filling up his pantry, then taking him out to dinner.

I remember one of our first arguments was over a bag of Doritos. On one grocery store outing, Mark tagged along, and was shocked when I tossed a full priced bag of Doritos into the cart. He couldn't believe I was so casual about buying a $4 bag of chips, something he never allowed himself. "What are you doing?" he blurted out. I remember staring at him like he was crazy. I just wanted to eat Doritos, what did he care? He also found it odd that I insisted upon wheeling the cart up and down every aisle, with no shopping list or plan about what to buy--just picking and choosing as I walked along. It was then I discovered that Mark bought about six items a week, and knew exactly where they were in the store. Six items! That was no way for a Princess to eat. I got my Doritos. Looking back, we can laugh about that now, yet in some ways it was a tiny blip on an important radar screen that we ignored. We never realized we handled money so differently and how this issue would play a huge role in our relationship and future.

We were in love, and despite Mark's initial life plans, we decided to marry even before graduating from college, at the young age of 21. I should tell you that to buy my engagement and wedding rings, Mark sold his beloved drum set. And it was just the first of many sacrifices he made for me.

Once when we were married, we

lived in a small student apartment. Thoughts about how to live never concerned us. We were together. We were young, full of dreams and energy. Anything was possible. And we didn't need much apart from each other. Or so we thought. Our wedding gift money kept us afloat for a while, and income from odd jobs. Mark tutored, I worked at a winery, and we were getting by. When we needed or wanted things out of reach of our cash flow, we found it easy to charge on credit cards, or I should say, I found it easy. Mark was not quite on board for the credit card life yet.

Mark finished out his last year at college as a magna cum laude with a double degree in math and economics, a wife, and Doritos in the cupboard (despite what he thought about my purchases). Following his graduation, we moved back to his hometown, and purchased a small house. Since Mark had been such an excellent student in college, he was awarded an internship at an actuarial firm where he got a job immediately after graduation. Credit was not hard to come by with his employment and income. Even though we had no idea how to handle credit cards, loans, how to budget, or plan about next year, let alone next month, we were offered credit and loans at every turn.

We just didn't worry,

or think much about money,

we always assumed we would have it.

IT TAKES TWO TO TANGO

{Summer 2002}

As evidenced by the Dorito incident, Mark was initially uneasy with my rather carefree spending habits. Never having lived without considering every purchase, he was again horrified by our first outing to Walmart as newlyweds, with my mother along, where I happily filled the shopping cart with $200 worth of "stuff" for our little apartment. When I went back the next day and charged another $200, he was very upset. A lot of what I bought seemed unnecessary to Mark, since he had never had or needed much. But I made it look so easy and fun. And my mother didn't seem to object, or think anything of it. Everything seemed possible. Our apartment filled up and looked cozy. As a new wife, I was so excited to make our home as warm and inviting as possible. Looking back at this now, I wasn't getting stuff to make it cozy, but rather buying stuff to make myself feel better. Jon Acuff says, *"You can't compare your beginning to some else's end."* Being a newlywed, I wanted to house to look like my parents, full of treasured items: my beginning to my parents' end. I was concerned, to an extent, about what other people thought of us being married so young, and I wanted to act the part as best as I could.

As is so often the case when couples marry, their values merge. Unfortunately, my spending habits were impacting our finances, and Mark was enjoying a freedom that he'd never known. I convinced him to open his first credit card. It was so easy just to slide that plastic card and go home with whatever we wanted or felt we needed. About two thirds of the way into our first year of marriage, we had spent up to the $3000 limit on our new, shiny black credit card. Of course we had every intention of paying it off quickly, but somehow, things always came up, and I just called into the credit card company and asked to "up" the limit. And they almost always said yes. Soon we were up to $5000 in debt, at 16% interest, on that one card alone.

By nature, I'm fun loving and easy going. That's in part what attracted Mark to me. But while he had been one to worry about money, and live on a shoestring, my breezy ways were rubbing off on him. The more we were together, the more he began to rationalize our habits and lifestyle.

When he felt uncomfortable with our spending, he just told himself: "This is what married couples do. This is what grown-ups do. We need to establish credit. I'm working, and working men use credit cards." And slowly, his mindset began to change. Mark was no longer living frugally, but rather, more impulsively. Reckless and irresponsible like me.

We were happy, enjoying life and each other, secure in the love of our families who lived close by, and the benefits of two incomes. Mark was working as an actuary, while I was a drug and alcohol counselor. These were our early married years without big responsibilities or children. Mark was finally allowing himself to enjoy the fruits of his labor. He worked, therefore he could spend. I worked too, so I did the same. Why did we feel like we 'deserved' a reward for our hard work? There seems to be a common thread among people who work and are in debt. What they don't see is that the true reward they can give themselves is to be debt free!

After a while, Mark stopped asking or noticing how much I used our credit cards. We were both caught up in a kind of materialism that was familiar to me, but new and enticing to Mark. Our mortgage was low, we had no children, we ate out frequently--we were living large. And then larger (or so we thought).

This was a dance we both enjoyed, but we didn't realize the long-term damage we were causing.

Digging a Big Hole

{Summer 2003}

After returning to Mark's hometown, I finished my studies and got my degree. Shortly after graduating, I began a job as a drug and alcohol counselor, which I held for a year and a half. It felt good to be using my degree and helping people; I had a vested interest because my brother was a drug addict and I wanted to help others like him. I enjoyed this job tremendously, but in November 2004 I discovered I was pregnant with our first child. I did not want to be working at that point, because I was burnt out at the job, so I stopped counseling.

It didn't take long, however, to realize that we were missing the income from my job, so in order to make some extra cash, I began working for a direct sales job that allowed me to work largely from home.

I've always had an outgoing personality and been blessed with the gift of gab, so I sold and sold, recruited and recruited, and was making some great money. Mark was proud of me and my success. So proud, in fact, that he agreed that I needed a better car than my 1994 Saturn, which was a wedding gift from my parents, meaning we didn't have any car payments. I was moving up quickly in my new career. Looks and status counted for a lot in this company's culture.

We decided on that Audi that Mark had once dreamed about. Why not? We were clever we thought, trading in my old Saturn to buy a used car, and getting all the luxury features that came with it--heated seats, mahogany trim, Bose speakers, and leather everywhere. As Mark loved to say, "It was a sweet car." But rather than buying with cash, we allowed ourselves to be talked into a car loan for the first time. We rationalized this loan, something that was going to become a bad habit over the next few years. What was another $260 a month to us? We were both doing well, and from all appearances, were successfully moving up our respective corporate ladders. The details of the loan were of little consideration-- higher rates for a used car, and more car than we really needed. But we were on our way. Would I do this now? Certainly not, but at the time it seemed like a good idea and we didn't think much about it.

I cannot blame the direct sales company for my spending. But a culture of superficiality and materialism infiltrated the work model. Look good, spend and spend-- it was largely about appearances, both personally and professionally, and it fed into my already materialistic side. I enjoyed dressing the part in my expensive outfits, showing up at sales events in my shiny Audi, and I was good at what I did. My customers and sales team loved me and my event planning. Sales events were parties, and everyone was having a good time, while I wracked up record numbers. At the end of one year, I was given a luxury car for my use. Now we had two fancy cars in our garage. We looked like we had it all together.

I must also add that I learned a great deal about business from this job--things that I have put to good use in my own company today. It tapped into the creative side of me that is one of my best qualities, along with my love of public speaking and event planning. In hindsight, I felt like I was getting an MBA on the run, but the price was high. Looking nice cost money, and I was too good at spending.

In August of 2005, I gave birth to our first child, a son. Mark and I felt incredibly blessed. Our family dreams were being fulfilled, and our careers were flourishing. From outward appearances, we had it all.

But I was still working for the direct sales company, and beginning to play the role of the high-powered career woman. In order to juggle work and motherhood, I decided I needed a nanny to help around the house and look after my son when I had work calls or events. Looking back at this decision, I think to myself "A nanny, that is so not me!" The reason I stopped working as a counselor was because I wanted to be a stay at home mom, then I find myself working more hours away from him than with him.

Then too, I decided I needed a secretary to handle my paperwork and bookkeeping. My income was good, but not THAT good. These decisions, to hire two assistants to allow me to grow in my career, were not really in line with my earnings. They were an extravagance. My expenses were growing way out of proportion to my earnings. And the expenses were so great that I was not able to enjoy my income as I had before. A big red flag was waving, but I failed to see it. Mark started noticing it, but ignored it. We never communicated about this until years later.

I should have seen it. But I rationalized again. I convinced myself that I needed the extra help to be successful. This was a new and bad habit. And one we'd pay for in short order.

By January of 2006, we had doubled our previous debt load in credit card payments and my student loans, and now, we had an additional $260 a month car payment, and salaries for my two assistants.

Our families had no idea what was going on in our financial lives. After all, we had a 'free' company car and a fancy Audi in the driveway. By all outwards appearances we looked like we were making a LOT of money every month. We didn't even grasp the severity of our situation yet, we just assumed we'd pay everything off with our next tax return, but then something else would come up. Like a vacation, or something else more important. Wasn't debt something other people just had? If we could keep it manageable then it wasn't such a big deal to us.

Looking back, I see the warning signs, the lack of communication, and the shame and embarrassment building up. Society tells us to pretend like everything is okay, but it is OKAY to talk about your financial problems. I think about what would have happened if we just stopped right here, and decided at this point to get out of debt once and for all.

But the hole was about to get deeper…

DEEPER IN

{Spring 2006}

Mark and I, along with our eight-month-old son, took a vacation to visit family in South Carolina. We enjoyed the change in scenery, the vitality of the area, and impulsively bought a house during our visit, a big, 3,200 square foot, $225,000.00 custom built home, with all the amenities designed to our specifications. The house we had always dreamed of, and decided to move there. We came home to tell our friends about our plans to move, ignoring the looks of shock on their faces. We had been in Upstate New York all our lives; the adventure of moving excited us.

We went to South Carolina as visitors with a $65,000 mortgage, and left as the new owners of a quarter of a million dollar house. We had no idea how we were going to afford this house, but we weren't worried.

Based on our two incomes, a bank offered us 100% of the money needed with no down payment! So what if we were moving from a $600 a month mortgage payment to a $1,700 payment? We were both doing well in our jobs, moving up in the world, and because of the nature of our work, could live anywhere in the country. We were swept up in the excitement, the possibility of having our dream house, made to order just for us. Mark's brothers and their families were excited about having us close by too, so this seemed like the right thing to do.

We thought about what the house would look like upon completion,(another moment of seeing the grandeur of stuff) and not about the cost of moving all our belongings from New York to South Carolina. No problem, just put it on a credit card. And furnishing that big house? Again, no problem-- furniture stores are always eager to offer those 0% down loans. So we bought furniture to fill in space that we'd never known in our little house back in New York. At the rate we were earning, we told ourselves we'd have those furniture loans paid off in no time. And for any little extras, we went cruising down the aisles of

Walmart, filling the cart with $1000 worth of "stuff" we needed on trip one, and $600 on the second trip, all charged on plastic. By now, Mark was used to this, and our lovely house "needed" so many things. I didn't want my new friends in South Carolina to see my house empty, so within a couple of months our house was completely filled with new furniture.

But a harsh reality hit soon after we moved into our new home. My job in sales, which had flourished in Upstate New York, was not doing as well in my new community. I'd left my client base, was not used to the Southern culture, and started watching my income drop, drastically. I loved this job because it allowed me to stay home with my young son (even though I had a nanny), but it was becoming apparent that the big bucks I'd previously earned were not happening here. I felt like a failure, but I still had my car and my looks, and was not one to give up easily.

I redoubled my efforts to sell. I spent money I didn't have, money I wasn't going to recoup, to throw events and parties for women who just didn't want my product as they had in New York. For the first time,

Mark and I began to argue about my job. He could see that I was throwing money away and sinking us into a big hole. But I just couldn't give up. I was so driven by the fear of failure that I ignored the severity of the situation that we were in. I wasn't looking at our current financial situation, but rather looking to what 'could be.' That is the dreamer in me, but when push came to shove, I was damaging our finances and I should have realized it then. Instead I planned *more* events, put hundreds of miles on my car to promote sales, losing more money and nothing was working. My marriage was being stressed in a way I was not used to. We argued, something not typical for us. Mark was always supportive, but this time, he was trying to be realistic. I was mad at him for not dreaming with me, but he was getting angrier and angrier at me, every month I continued our finances got worse.

Again, I want to emphasize that the company I was worked for was not to blame for my failure in South Carolina. Circumstances and timing were just not in my favor. I continued my job in sales because I was too prideful to quit. I didn't understand why God would allow me to be successful at something, and then have it taken away so quickly. I figured it was something I must be doing, so I continued to try and make it work.

For those who think this is an easy fix, it isn't. It takes determination, patience, and sacrifice. And Mark and I just weren't there yet. We couldn't say NO to ourselves. Just at the point where we were turning a corner in the right direction, we'd fall back on old ways. Our credit card safety nets. Our very own false sense of financial security.

We even had thoughts of claiming bankruptcy, but were smart enough to see that if we did that, we would be right back in the same financial situation we were in if we didn't change our behaviors. Bankruptcy is not the easy fix that it seems, especially if you don't change the spending habits that got you into your first financial mess.

THE DEVIL'S IN THE DEALS

{Winter 2006}

Temptation came endlessly in the mail, in the form of credit card offers. Mark, despite his frugal upbringing, was quick to see the angles, and he got good at playing the credit card games. When an offer for an American Express card came in the mail to our South Carolina house, in December of 2007, he took it. His rationalization this time-- AmEx made you pay off the balance; it would force us to stay honest, to make our payments. But the charges if you were late were harsh. We believed we could control this card, this time; *this time it would be different.*

And the best bonus came with this card. If we got it with the promotion in December, we'd get an instant 50,000 extra points, which equated to $500 in gift cards at various stores. Mark wanted to build a deck, and to do that, he needed a table saw. Problem solved. Get the card; get a "free" table saw. So he signed on the dotted line, and our house was on its way to a new deck, but we couldn't afford the lumber yet. Then, since we paid off the first few payments on time and in full with my waitressing paychecks, we got a second offer. Spend X amount of money, and get another $500 in points towards another purchase of our choice. Bingo! We bought the lumber using the second $500 gift card and we had a deck up in a few months. My talented husband provided all the labor. We told ourselves that we'd recoup that investment if we ever sold the house. The deck felt like it had been free, but of course, it wasn't because we had to spend money on that card to earn the points, and now we had even more debt. The devil was always in those deals.

But, we still didn't get honest with ourselves, and when I was having dental problems that Spring, the American Express card came to the rescue once again. It turned out I needed a root canal and a crown, costing about $3,500, which we did not have in cash. Nor did we have the available credit on any other card because they were all maxed out. So we put it on the AmEx, and my dental work was taken care of.

It all seemed to be working, but we were just fooling ourselves. By this time, we were having trouble making American Express payments in full and on time. The fines and fees for such mistakes were killers. We had just fallen into another credit card trap, fallen back into an old habit. This became a pattern, and a cycle that repeated itself several times before we were ready to make a life change. And at this point, we still weren't there yet.

We were sinking deeper and deeper into debt, all the while telling ourselves that we were gaining control of our spending. Or so we pretended to have control, we didn't want to go without.

To give you an ideal of what our cycle looked like: we'd get excited about paying off debt, work hard at it for a few months. Then we'd reward ourselves for our hard work by going out to an expensive restaurant or buying a new laptop computer. Then we would get a few more bills and realize that we needed to start getting out of debt again, we would try hard for a few months, and then slip right back into our old spending habits. We would get a 0% credit card offer, switch all our credits cards to that one and forget to close the old one. It was a vicious cycle.

The person I am now is shaking my head. What were we doing? Why did we ever think we were winning switching between credit card companies and signing up for those shiny bonus offers? The credit card companies always win, but make you *think* you are. And the situation we put ourselves in is all too commonplace in our society. It just takes many of us a long time to realize the dangers hiding in those little plastic cards.

MY FAILURE EXPOSED

{January 2007}

Our life looked good from the outside but was quickly turning into a real nightmare. With all our hopes of a new life in South Carolina crumbling, my job in direct sales falling flat, and our inability to get away from our spiraling debt, we were in crisis. At 27 years old, we had over $40,000.00 in debt: a huge mortgage, college loans, car payments, credit card debt, and bills piling up every month. This is the night when we sat down in our lovely bedroom, that fateful night of reckoning, and spread out all the bills and expenses, we knew we were in serious trouble.

I was crying.

Mark was numb.

In addition to all the bills and credit cards strewn around us, we were facing a $1000 deficit a month. Despite some half-hearted attempts to stick to some sort of budget, we were still struggling to change our ways. It was no easy task.

I was still trying to make my sales job work, and a few days after our heart-to-heart on the bed, Mark wanted to talk to me about it. He told me that he wanted me to quit, he was sick of losing money every month and having me be so stressed out. I wanted to prove to him that I could turn my job around and make it work, so I decided (against his will) to give the job one more week. More events, more money lost to refreshments, deals, gas and giveaways, and still, no gains. In fact I LOST around $2,000 dollars that week.

Driving home from this disastrous sales event, I started to cry. And in my despair, I prayed asking God for help and a sign, something to tell me what to do next. I needed to work, my family needed my income, but this was obviously not going to be the way. Suddenly on the radio, the song, "Does Anybody Hear Her?," by the Christian group, Casting Crowns, started playing. The lyrics felt like they were written just for me: "She's driving 100 miles in the wrong direction." I knew at that moment deep down in my heart that God was sending me a sign that I was working toward the wrong goal. This job was leading me in the wrong direction from where he wanted me to go.

When I got home, I told Mark I was done with the direct sales job, changed my clothes into a professional suit, and went directly to a high-end steakhouse to apply as a server. My determination and personality helped again--I got the job. But the price was high. This was an establishment where 99% of the servers were men, and I was the newbie. And my hours--from 3:00 pm until midnight, were grueling, not to mention diametrically opposed to my family's hours. The work was hard, I was an "outsider," and many times felt like I was pledging a fraternity with the challenges they put me though. They had no idea they were dealing with a woman who was very determined and headstrong, one that they could not break. The hours were a shock from my previous job, where I could work largely from home and around my family's needs. But it was a job, and we needed the money. Also, I desperately wanted to contribute to my family, and not leave Mark to shoulder the burden alone. I had so much shame at the financial situation I felt I had gotten us into. We were both stressed, but now, at least, a bit of relief was in sight.

Since I decided to quit my job in direct sales, I had to call and tell my company of my decision. I also had to arrange for them to pick up my luxury company car. This was a huge blow to my ego. I loved that car, and what I believed it represented--my success in a big corporation, my personal talent in working with people, and my gift in sales. But after those four months in South Carolina, when I realized I was no longer making a viable income, I had to let it go. This was another moment of reckoning.

I don't know what I expected when the car was to be taken. But the events of that day will always be etched in my mind-shame, embarrassment, and public exposure. Instead of having the option of dropping the car off, I learned that the car would be taken from the driveway of my custom home in broad daylight (at 4:30 p.m., no less), when my neighbors would all be coming home from work. No small tow truck came, but instead, a huge, noisy, flatbed vehicle so big that it actually blocked traffic on our street. It looked horribly out of place in our suburban family neighborhood, and as it bellowed its way up to our house, it made such a racket that my neighbor's kids came out to witness my latest nightmare. The car was loaded up in what seemed like an hour, with more noise and commotion, while I sat, hiding in my upstairs bedroom, behind closed curtains, leaving Mark downstairs to turn over they keys to the driver.

As the flatbed drove away, the crowd of kids who were now part of this circus jumped on bikes and skateboards and grabbed onto the back of the truck while it rumbled down the street. It was humiliating and humbling. My pride was in a heap on the floor. I had hit rock bottom. Until this moment I had been able to hide our financial mess, now I had nowhere to hide. Was I ready to stand up and admit that I had a problem with money? Was I prepared to be exposed? I didn't have a choice, all of my secrets were out. I was horrible with money, my car had just been towed away, and everyone saw it. That night on the bed was hard, but it was just Mark and me. This was out in the open, for everyone to see and judge.

SACRIFICE

{Spring 2007}

Sacrifice was something that I had to do by working at that steakhouse every night. Mark and I slipped back into some old habits again, habits that had gotten us into the very trouble we were trying to dig out of. I was tired, so we ate out more. Food we bought at the grocery store spoiled, when night after night Mark would take our son out for fast food or make boxed mac and cheese, and I would grab something on the dark ride home. And we had a little more money, so rather than putting it all toward paying off our large debt, we decided we deserved some rewards for our hard work. We started spending again. Turning to our old ways of buying things we wanted, and justifying those expenses. You may be starting to see a pattern here: little self-control over how we 'felt' about our finances. We got what we wanted, felt like we deserved a break because we had made a little progress. One step forward, two steps back. That was the game we kept on playing.

We'd use Mark's bonuses from work, my restaurant tips, or a tax refund, to pay off some debt, but not quite all, feel like we were on the right track, and start charging again. Not to mention, we never got to enjoy Mark's bonuses, or my new income. It was all going to pay more and more interest on loans, and the cycle continued.

We were starting to realize that we had to sacrifice our needs and wants…that was not an easy idea to grasp.

THE SLOW CLIMB OUT

{Summer 2007}

Despite all the crises that we found ourselves in, Mark and I held fast to one another and to our faith. We'd lost our way financially, but our core values, while shaken, were still intact. We loved each other, we loved our son, and we wanted to do the right and responsible thing with our lives.

By the summer of 2007, we felt we were on our way. Mark's job was always steady, but his income was not enough to get us out of our mess. I was working as a server at an upscale restaurant, and bringing home $100 to $200 a night. But we were still deep into debt.

Like ships passing in the night, our schedules were opposite, and I felt like I was losing touch with the rhythm of my son's daily life--his favorite breakfast, what he ate for dinner, what books he enjoyed reading at night, what it felt like to give him his bath before bedtime and tuck him in. My new job was providing a positive income flow, but it left little time for our family, and that had always been a priority for Mark and me.

In addition, we were under some of the worst stress we'd ever experienced in our marriage. I was exhausted; Mark was doing double duty working full time at his job and tending to our son's needs alone, at night. I look back with amazement at how we got through this period, but one thing I was determined to do was never to let Mark think that he was alone in his despair during this difficult time. He became depressed, and I did all I could to cheer him up.

In my times of despair and weakness, I turned to God for guidance, and he would always ask the same questions of me, "Do you trust me in this time of trial? and "Do you trust me enough to do what it will take to get out of debt?" And my answer was always, "Yes, I'm trying to." I'd fall down and get up, over and over again. But God's message was always the same, and that sustained me.

By nature, I am wired to be optimistic; I wanted to help contribute to getting out of this financial mess, and I dug down deep for solutions. I also turned to the Bible for guidance, to I Peter, (Chapter 3, Verse 4), which encourages a wife to support her husband, "by behavior," and "have a heart that is gentle and quiet. That will not wear out." I believe in this role of a wife with her husband, and worked to brighten Mark's spirits. I prayed for him constantly, and encouraged him when I could have discouraged him. I let him lead our family, and prayed for God to give him the strength to do it. We had always been a team, sometimes with one having to carry the ball more than the other. But we kept our balance, and never resorted to the blame game. Too often I've seen that happen with couples in the same situation, and the reality is that both people have a role in their situation. We live by the motto "we got into this together, now we have to get out by working together."

I always knew that we had different strengths that complemented one another. Mark was deliberate, thoughtful, steady, and artistic; I was spontaneous, fun-loving, and energetic, sometimes a bit headstrong, but always full of ideas. We each had our own position in the family, and were comfortable in our roles. But now I allowed Mark to take the lead in any place he could feel empowered. I saw him as head of the household. After all, it was his steady job that provided us our greatest security. Through all this, he put on a suit and tie and reported to work every day. I respected him greatly, and despite my own fear, was rarely negative, never talked to friends or family about our financial problems, and never complained to him or put him down. As Paul wrote to husbands in his letter to the Ephesians, "Each one of you must love his wife as he loves himself and the wife must respect her husband." (NIV: Ephesians 5:33). I have always believed that this is the core of a strong marriage. I wanted to show Mark how much I loved him through the respect I gave him.

And out of this crisis, our love and marriage grew stronger, when it could have easily been torn apart. Slowly, and as a team, we began to face our fears, to own up to our weaknesses, our indulgence in material things, and the mess we had made of our finances. And we turned to our faith over and over again, to keep us on a steady course to rebuild our lives.

It was finally time for us to admit that we were just plain sick of worrying about money, sweating out every bill, living from paycheck to paycheck, being afraid to go the mailbox, and all just to keep our heads above water. It filled our days and nights, and was sapping our energy and spirits. I hated my job, and wanted to be a stay-at-home-mom, but at the same time, I wanted to contribute to the financial well being of our family, and help clean up our mess. For the first time, we had to stop, take a hard look at our lifestyle and spending habits, and honestly admit that we had allowed our spending to spin out of control.

We knew we needed help. Before, we weren't really ready to do the hard work of repair, but this time believed we were. And we went at it with renewed energy and hope. No more excuses, no more rationalizations. We started to give up things that we weren't willing to give up before. We were committed to changing for good.

And most importantly, we decided to live on cash only. We knew this was key to making a sea change in our spending habits. I took out envelopes, labeled them each with a major category--groceries, clothing, gas, cell phone, utilities, etc. I cashed Mark's next paycheck, and divided up the money accordingly. When an envelope was empty, we simply had to wait until the next paycheck. It provided the reality check that we just didn't have the discipline for, since we'd fallen into bad habits. Now, we were going to break those, for once and for all. And it was a challenge that was both frightening and liberating.

For the next year and a half, we cut whatever we could. We limited ourselves to $50 a week for groceries, accomplishing this by learning how to meal plan and use coupons. Got rid of our cable T.V. subscription keeping only the basic channels; Mark sacrificed his sports and would only watch them if they were on those basic channels. We also got rid of our land line, and kept only one cell phone on the least expensive plan possible. We never ate out, had to end our date nights, took no vacations, became a one-car family, and bought only the necessities. If we needed clothes, we went to thrift shops or garage sales. We even rented out a room in our house to bring in additional income--and this time the money went to pay off debt. What was strange is that we started hanging out with friends who didn't have much money in our attempt to shy away from saying no to more expensive pastimes. Was this a way to hide, or a way to stay strong?

Holidays, birthdays, anniversaries, and Christmas were especially hard times, but we stuck to our plan as best we could. We didn't buy presents for each other, only our son. In order to get him a special toy he wanted for Christmas, we would sell things online through EBay or Craig's List. On one special occasion, I wanted to get him a GeoTrax Train Set. He didn't ask for much, but this was something he wanted for his birthday, so I held a garage sale, raised $75, and got him the set. There was even enough money left over to buy a pizza, a luxury at that point. And I had stuck to our "cash only" resolution. This was very hard, but we were so determined to make this change. It had gotten to the point that the pain of staying in debt was greater than the pain of making a big change in our lifestyle. Even thought this was hard to do, staying in debt and ignoring it had become the harder task.

Looking around online, I discovered some consumer focus groups and began participating in their marketing questionnaires, earning $3.00 a survey. It seemed too good to be true, but I did my research and found out that many people did this. Those little checks added up, and the look on the bank teller's face when I went to cash a $3.00 check was priceless. Nothing was too small if it could help my family. I realized I could find creative ways out of my problems, and it felt good. One year I saved up enough money doing these surveys that I was able to pay for 80% of our Christmas shopping*! That was a huge burden lifted from our shoulders.

Sacrifice, drastic life changes, bare bones living. But given the depth of our debt (at a relatively young age), this is what had to be done. It wasn't easy, and Mark and I were both under great stress--but determined.

To be honest, we slipped occasionally and would go out to dinner instead of paying down credit cards or ignore our budget one week because we forgot to get cash out. This process is hard, and we aren't perfect. But slowly, we found our mindset changing. And that was the beginning for us. We were slowing down enough to finally take stock of what we valued, and it wasn't the big house or the fancy cars. One night, Mark confessed that he didn't even know why he'd wanted that Audi so much. To prove what? To show off his success at work? To be an extension of himself? And at what cost? Thousands of dollars in payments and repairs. This was not who he was. His mindset was changing.

A luxury car was not a value anymore.

Financial responsibility, doing the things he loved doing with me and our son, feeling free from constant worry, these were now the values that he was rediscovering. At last we were on the same page. Most importantly, we started to realize something else that has become key--our spending was becoming a reflection of the things we valued most.

MORE TRIALS, A SMALL VICTORY & A BLESSING

{Fall 2007 – Summer 2009}

In the midst of our financial collapse, Mark and I were having personal tragedies of another sort. I had a 15-month-old son when we moved into our house in South Carolina, and we were hoping to have many more children. That had always been our dream. To our joy, we discovered shortly after moving in, that I was pregnant, but this time, complications arose and I suffered a miscarriage in the first trimester. These were trying times for Mark and me in so many ways, but somehow, we held on. My fertility problems continued for a year and a half, and I wondered how we could bear yet another disappointment.

The thought of not being able to have more children greatly saddened Mark and me, but fortunately, surgery solved my problem. And in the Spring of 2008, I discovered I was pregnant again. I was getting used to doing without, in so many ways, and here we were with the promise of the greatest of gifts--another child.

We were also beginning to make headway into lowering our once seemingly insurmountable debt, and things were definitely looking up. Then, 28 weeks into my pregnancy, I got a letter from the IRS, informing us that we were going to be audited, and because of the large discrepancy in my deductions from the previous year, the letter stated that we owed them $17,000.00. I felt stunned and defeated, and called Mark in tears. This would set us back, and we had been working so hard.

I was panicking, but Mark remained calm, and called our accountant. As it turned out, this was a bit of a scare tactic, to get folks to pay if they didn't want the hassle of fighting the IRS and proving their case. And while my "write offs" were dramatically different from the previous tax year, there was a paper trail that proved our case was legitimate. Of course it took one full year to pull together all the needed papers and documents, but fortunately I'd kept records. This extra work was not what I needed at this time, still juggling my family's needs, and my pregnancy, but I hunkered down and did it.

In the end, we only had to pay $3,500.000, a hard-won victory. We were able to borrow that amount, plus the accountant's fee, from Mark's parents. More debt, yes, but not $17,000 worth. This still set us back $3,500, so it was a bit of a blow, but we dusted ourselves off and went back at it. And we were fortunate to have his parents and their generosity to turn to, something we tried not to do, but this time, we had no other option. And we paid them back quickly. Time and time again we were knocked down, but we kept getting back up and pushing forward.

In June of 2009, I gave birth to a beautiful, healthy daughter. This was such a blessing after the trials and hardships of the previous three years. Slowly, our debt was diminishing, and at the same time, our family was growing.

SCISSORS AND COUPONS

{Winter 2008}

By the end of thirteen months, Mark and I were still cutting everywhere and chipping away at our mountain of debt. This was a rough time for us, and for our marriage, and I wanted to make a change to help hold the fabric of our family more closely together. I desperately wanted to quit the server job and be a stay-at-home-mom, but we needed my income.

After looking over our budget, Mark and I saw that the one major area we were not making much of a dent in, although we were trying, was groceries. And it was a biggie, because I saw it as something that I could decrease immediately. Necessity made me creative. I never thought of myself as being good with money, I knew I had a weak financial backbone, but I had to find a solution to this dilemma--I wanted to be home with my children and at the same time, be a financially contributing spouse.

So I challenged myself. If I could make up the difference we needed by clipping coupons and reducing our grocery bill from $1000 a month to $200 a month, I wouldn't just be saving money, I'd be making a wage. If it would work, I could stop waitressing. This was a huge incentive, and I went at it with a passion that surprised even Mark.

I went to school on couponing, read and researched everything I could get my hands on. I learned about the tricks of the trade,* planned meals around deals*, and worked every angle of the coupon world. All during this time, I was still taking care of my son, my house and waitressing from 3 p.m. until midnight, but I saw a light at the end of the tunnel, and was determined to make it work. The more I got into it, the more I felt it was possible. As it turned out, it was not only possible, but very workable, and after two months, I got pretty good at it. A fanatic! It wasn't uncommon to see me on the floor of the Rite Aid store with my coupon binder spread out, searching for some coupon or other. I never went anywhere without my stash of clippings, and went to extremes to save more and more. The planning and organization of a shopping trip could take hours, in some cases two days--cutting coupons, reading newspaper flyers, going online and checking store deals.

As the weeks went by, I realized that my plan was working. After two months, in March of 2008, I quit my steak house job to stay home with my son. I had been working outside the house for 13 months, and I now felt confident that I was ready to meet my challenge—to be a better steward of the finances God had given us. The timing of this was also fortunate, because it allowed me to stop waitressing before my daughter, Hannah, was born. I was able to be home full time with my son and newborn baby, and things felt right for the first time in years.

Coupon shopping trips with young children became yet another challenge. On one especially memorable day, I set out with my three-year-old son and my six-week-old daughter in tow. As with so many of my initial efforts, this proved to be both a disastrous and comical adventure. I had spent 6-7 hours planning this shopping trip. I actually had so many deals in hand that it was going to take three transactions to complete all my purchases, since stores limit the number of coupons-per-trip allowed. And this was going to be a cash only affair, in keeping with my new financial resolution.

So off we went to the local grocery store, with coupons and transactions mapped out--my battle plan in hand. After shopping for an hour and a half, I arrived at the cash register. My son had begun to get cranky midway through our "adventure," so I got him some Goldfish crackers, and he happily scarfed them down. By the time they rang up my purchases and discounted my coupon savings, I had purchased $451 of groceries and household items for $51.00! I did it! But then, opening my purse to take out my wallet, I realized that in all my planning, I had forgotten the cash. No cash, no checkbook, and no credit card!

I was in shock--in one moment I felt triumphant, in the next, totally deflated. It didn't help that by now my daughter was screaming, and the cashier was upset, probably at the thought of all that time wasted punching in my coupons, and the thought of having to put all these items back on the shelves. She ripped the empty

Goldfish bag out of my son's hands, and he turned to me as we left the store, foodless, crying loudly, "Why don't you have any money to feed us?" Everyone was staring at us in pity. I not only suffered the stigma of the mother who needs coupons to feed her family, but had two screaming children, no food, and no money. At that moment I felt like someone had stripped me of my Mother of the Year award. I was embarrassed, but determined to make it all work out. For the first time, I didn't care about being embarrassed.

And we went back. I drove the 10 minute trip home, got my money, and returned to claim my food. Despite all the work and embarrassment, it was worth it. My kids had food, I was under budget, and my pantry was full. Finding ways to save money was my new job, and I took it very seriously. As with all new endeavors, there is a learning curve, and I was willing to make mistakes to keep learning ways to carve an income out of coupon savings.

I began to share some of my methods with friends on Facebook, and then a few asked if I would teach them how my "coupon system" worked. There are many couponing women out there, but my friends were inspired by my success. This was a taste of what later became a kind of mission for me. I found that I enjoyed these sessions, as they grew from just a few friends in my living room to church assemblies where hundreds would gather to hear me talk. I began to tell my story, and word spread.

I found that the skills I had honed at the direct sales job were just as useful here. I love public speaking and sharing ideas with other moms. But this time, unlike my sales job, where I encouraged women to spend money, I was teaching them about living frugally and saving money in all areas of their lives.

A seed was planted, and I reached out further and further to help those who'd experienced similar financial problems. This was the direction I was meant to go in. This is where my personal challenge, my couponing, and my determination to help contribute to my family was leading me--on the path God had directed me toward that night, when I heard the "Casting Crowns" song on the radio.

I still pinch myself when I recall the journey that led me to this place. The sacrifices Mark, my children, and I made over the past year and a half were beginning to pay off. But we still had work to do to get financially fit.

MOVING FORWARD

{Fall 2009}

At this point, we'd been in South Carolina for three years, and while I was getting used to the Southern culture, Mark never truly felt at home there. Perhaps he'd grown disenchanted, but in any case, he was homesick for New York. To worsen matters, his brothers and their families decided to move back to their hometown in Upstate New York, and we were dealing with the loss of no longer living near family.

Mark was always missing visiting our friends, parents and siblings, he realized how important it was to him to be near his family and mine. And the clincher--the economy in the Charlotte area was in trouble, and the housing market in our neighborhood collapsed. We held our breath as one house after another on our street fell into foreclosure. If we did want to move, we'd have a hard time selling our big house in this declining market, and losing money was the last thing we needed at this point.

I was finally enjoying staying home with my son, being the proverbial soccer mom, and feeling more and more confident in my couponing work. For once, I was content and fulfilled in my life. But I had to consider Mark's feelings in this, and I prayed long and hard, asking God once again for a sign-- "If you want us to move back to New York, please make it obvious." And like the song on the radio, a sign did come.

Mark had changed jobs several months after arriving in South Carolina. Same line of work, but a different company in Charlotte. It was the sign-on-bonus from that job that helped us pay off our Audi, and that felt like a huge step for us. During the "audit" crisis, and five days after the birth of our daughter, Mark got word that his company was being bought out. And then in another huge stroke of good fortune, on that same day, Mark got a call from his former boss in New York, asking, "What can I do to get you back here?" It was exactly what Mark needed, and just in time.

And then another miracle. Our house was approved for a short sale. Ten houses around us were going into foreclosure, and we were already underwater in our mortgage (owing more than what we could sell it for). Eight weeks later it sold, with a cash deal, ensuring a quick closing. The bank covered the amount that we were underwater with and we had dodged the foreclosure bullet. We were able to get out with our credit and dignity intact, and began packing.

We counted ourselves blessed, but now we faced a new hurdle. Moving costs money, and we had nothing extra to spend. But I had learned to take advantage of every deal out there, and my strength surprised me. Rather than going to the big boys, the Mayflowers and United Van Lines, I found a do it yourself company called ABF U Pack. I negotiated the price of the move down to $1,200.00. We had to put that amount on a credit card, but it felt like we had just been granted a huge miracle in our house selling. We knew we had the tools and determination to pay off that $1,200 when we got home. After a lot of wrapping, packing, and sweating, we were on our way, with a four-year-old and three-month-old along for the ride.

HOME AGAIN

{Fall 2009}

By the time we left South Carolina in October 2009, we had cut our debt in half. We believed we were finally on the right track to getting out from underneath our financial burdens. We had tried and failed several times to get out of debt and stop using our credit cards but this time, we were absolutely determined.

For the first three weeks, we moved in with my sister, and had most of our belongings in boxes in a storage unit. We felt homeless. By November of that year, we found a very small townhouse, and moved once again. This time, however, we lived frugally. Sacrifices were made on a large and small scale. We sold almost everything we had to pay down debt and pay for our living expenses, keeping only a couch, two dressers, and three mattresses which we set on the floors of the bedrooms. We borrowed a table and two chairs for the kitchen from Mark's parents. Mark sold his prized drums (AGAIN)--Maple DW's, that he had purchased to replace the ones he sold to buy my engagement ring seven years prior. I was not as emotionally attached to things as some people are, but I did have a valuable antique ironstone collection and finally sold the little, milky white pitcher that was the last of the set I had kept. By now, we let our friends and family know about our debt. They were confused about why we were taking so many drastic measures; one of them actually asked, "Don't you think you downsized too much?" We wanted them to be along on our debt free journey now too. We were embarrassed to tell them, but so excited when many of them jumped on board and started working to pay off their debts too.

The first night in our new small townhome was strangely magical however. The heat hadn't been turned on yet, and we went to Walmart and bough two red coffee mugs because our boxes were not out of storage yet (we needed coffee!). After putting our kids to bed (we did have electric heaters in the bedrooms), Mark and I sat at the borrowed table in kitchen and drank coffee together. We had almost nothing from our former lives. All of our luxury items were gone, but it was an amazing moment. We had a place to live, and we could afford to do so. We were finally ready to tackle our mess. This is when we knew our mindsets had changed. We knew, this time, we would succeed in getting to our goal--financial responsibility.

The townhouse was 800 square feet, so small that it was almost comical. My kitchen appliances were on a shelf in the one car garage, so whenever I needed to cook, I had to make a trip outside, a not so fun trip in the winter months. The table and chairs almost completely filled the kitchen, and to get into the refrigerator, I had to move the table and my chair out of the way--not too convenient in the middle of a meal when someone wanted more milk, or something I'd forgotten to take out ahead of time. To operate the portable dishwasher, it had to be rolled out into the middle of the kitchen and be plugged into the sink. And the bathroom was so tiny I could sit on the toilet seat, take the clothes out of the dryer and fold them on the spot. What convenience! The biggest problem with the upstairs bathroom, however, was not even its size. It was our children who inadvertently made the discovery.

Every morning, at the same time, our son would wake up early in his bedroom, adjacent to the bathroom. We tried moving him to our daughter's room, and her into his, but then she too started waking at the same time, early in the morning, crying. This in turn made the teenagers living on the opposite side of our daughter's room pound the wall in anger, further heightening her crying distress. Coincidentally, these times were those when Mark and I took our showers--early in the morning before work. Finally, after playing musical beds with our sleeping arrangements, we found that the walls were so thin around the bathroom shower and toilet, that the sound of the shower flowing or the toilet flushing was like that of a Mack Truck plowing though the house. Mark and I wound up in the room closest to the pounding plumbing, and we all eventually slept, sort of, though the night.

With all this, we were still working our way out of debt. We had cut it down to $15,000.00, and we were continually coming up with ways to save money. I was still doing my little consumer surveys. Most of the $3.00 checks I received from those went into the house savings account, but every once in a while, I'd cash one check and treat myself to a Dunkin Donuts coffee. It felt like such a luxury! We were living bare bones lean, sometimes frustrated, but always determined. We loved to entertain, but our house was so small we couldn't even enjoy the simple pleasure of having friends over. Christmas was tight, both space wise and financially. Again we only bought gifts for our children, and we could barely fit a Christmas tree into our little townhouse, but we finally found one small enough to squeeze in.

By this time, Mark and I were completely in sync regarding our finances. It took a while for me to understand why he wanted to do spreadsheets, and it took him a while to understand why I needed a clothing budget every month (kids grow you know!). We were both on the same page in terms of spending, saving, and living a cash only life. And that December of 2009, we made a decision that insured we could not slip back into our old habits that had brought us to this point. At the kitchen table, we took all our credit cards, some paid off and some not and ran them through the shredder.

SHREDDING PLASTIC

As we sat watching our credit cards coming out of the shredder in little plastic strips, we knew there was no turning back. After trying and failing many times to stick to financial resolutions, we knew we had to do something to break our old pattern for once and for all. Done. No more game playing. No more falling back on old habits. We had removed the "safety net," eliminated the "emergency fund." There could be no more rationalizing why we needed to keep them. We were going to live on cash. Experts say it takes 21 days to break and make habits. Our spending had become a habit. So to break the cycle, we had to take this leap of faith.

Many think that this might have felt wonderful, even something to celebrate. But the truth is, it wasn't a joy we felt as we watched our cards shredding to bits; it was fear. Could we really do it this time, really live within our means? What would we do for Christmas, birthdays, holidays? What if our house needed a huge repair? What if our car broke down? What if we had an emergency? Regardless, we knew we had to get out of this crushing debt. And it was the *only* way we felt we could achieve this goal. We had tried and failed repeatedly to be financially responsible. We always intended to pay back our cards on time, in full, and used money from bonuses, windfalls, gifts, and the sale of many of our belongings, to make dents in our mountain of credit. But then for some reason, name a dozen, we'd go back onto a card again, and be right back to square one.

More debt.

More worry.

And until we truly changed our mindset about money, we fell into the traps that ensnare so many people who use credit without thinking. When we 'wanted' something, we'd rationalize, "what's another $50 on a credit card that's already up to

$14,000?" And as the balances grew and grew, even making a dent seemed impossible, so we'd say, we'll start again tomorrow. But this time, it was tomorrow. We were there.

With our partnership, faith in the belief that this was the right thing to do, we had made it to this point. We were going to live without plastic. To live on cash. To live within our means. And in the following months, we'd find out just what that meant.

I AM THAT LADY.COM

{Winter 2009}

Now that we had vowed to live on cash, I needed to find a way to help my husband provide for my growing family even more. I had begun couponing in South Carolina in 2008 to allow me to quit a waitressing job and stay home with my son. And I was successful. But back in Upstate New York, I was shocked to find that the online resources I had used to maximize my couponing system were not available. I had to "reinvent the wheel" so to speak, and began taking all I'd learned in Charlotte to recreate the resources I'd had there. I spent hours looking for local store coupon match-ups, and where to find the best deals. And it was then I realized that in doing this for my family, it only made sense to share it with others.

I believe that I went through my struggles for a reason, and with God's guidance, I was finally going "in the right direction." If I took my knowledge and used it to help others, I'd ultimately fulfill my promise to God, not to waste the experience I'd gained. I could help my community by providing a resource that was lacking. And since I was still crawling my way out of our financial mess, I knew the need for this help. I could benefit others, and it felt right. I kept teaching classes on couponing, showing women how to maximize their money by finding the best deals in local stores and online, how to organize coupons, how to use match-ups, "peelies," "blinkees," online coupon sites, and other tricks of the trade.

Then I realized that if I created a website, I could reach even more women. Luckily for me, I had taken a course in college on HTML, and knew the basics of designing a website. It was a beginning. Even more fortunately for me, the professor just happened to be Mark's brother, a web programmer, so I had a technical support expert in the family, just a phone call away!

One big obstacle facing me was that I needed $300 to get my website up and running. How could I do this and keep in line with my new financial resolutions of staying debt free? My solution: I held one large couponing seminar and charged a small fee to attend. This event raised $300, exactly what I needed to start my website, and I was able to start up I Am That Lady.com , 100% debt free!

People often ask how I came up with my website's name. One thing I love about my site is that it is a true reflection of me--silly, sassy, and bubbling with ideas and tips about how a mom can contribute to her family's financial needs. While washing dishes one night, I realized I was, as the cliché goes, "just that lady," the slightly crazy one in the store who backs up the line at the register with her kids and her pile of coupons. Just a mom with four kids in tow, trying to stretch her dollars further, running errands, keeping a household intact, and actually having a good time in the process. "I Am That Lady" said it all. And that was it. I filed for the URL name, and was on my way.

I am not about perfection, I actually despise that word. I'm about being practical, learning about money in an empowering way, and helping women like myself get through the day with some tips, a few laughs, and a lot of faith. As visitors flocked to my website, I realized that this was appealing to many moms out there--those of us who don't always have it together, but somehow manage to get meals on the table, keep the house relatively clean, and juggle a dozen balls in the air at once.

As I got more and more into my website, I added more features: recipes, "do it yourself" projects, meal planning ideas, tips on frugal living, and hot daily deals around town. Then too, I found myself rediscovering some of my interests in color, design, crafting, and began to recycle items found at garage sales into playful decorations for our house. All this was tapping into a creative energy that fueled my work, and I loved it.

In this process, I was developing a skill that I'd always admired in Mark--discipline. And that discipline helped me hone my mission. I not only learned to budget my money, but also my time, and that allowed me to better help others, while being available to my family and their growing needs.

GROWING ON ALL FRONTS

{Summer 2010}

My success with the website was helping me reach my goals, especially of helping others who found themselves drowning in debt. Until now, I had never thought of myself as being good with money. I knew I could sell in my days as a director in the corporate world, but making money and handling it was another. But I was learning as I went along. The old saying, "Necessity is the mother of invention" comes to mind, for as I faced my new frugal lifestyle, I found myself thinking of creative ways to save and make money. Couponing was key to starting me on this path, but as I worked to imagine ways to contribute to my family, I began to tap into inner resources that I'd never even realized were there.

Good thing too, because another challenge was looming. My son was about to enter preschool, and Mark and I decided that we wanted him to attend a private Christian school in our town. While it was a priority for us to give our kids a Christian education, it would add another $350 a month to our budget; we couldn't afford it but it was something we valued, and would sacrifice for. I considered going back to a job outside the house, but that went against everything I had worked for. Instead, I decided to try to make money from blogging, something I'd heard about. And I'd built up enough momentum on my website to believe it might be possible. As with couponing, I went at this with a passion that at times, I'm sure, made me look a little crazy. And when I get like that, things happen. Mark and I jokingly refer to this period as "the crazy years," but his belief in my passion urged me forward.

I spent hours putting together online mini courses and more "how to" videos on all aspects of frugal living. With the patient help of my brother-in-law, I retooled my website, learned about getting advertising and making money doing the thing I loved, teaching people. Things started to click, and more and more people were coming on board. It took me one year to build to the point where I was making a substantial income. I worked mostly at night after my children were in bed, or during nap times. The income first paid for my son's education but eventually I began exceeding his tuition and was able to help pay off some of our debt. And I never would have imagined, those many years ago when I worked for the direct sales company, that I'd have my own business now, and even expand enough to hire employees. All of this proves that a person can turn his or her life around with determination, faith, and the help of others, and in my case, the support of a wonderful husband.

As my website grew, so did my network, and I was asked to do some public speaking. I pinch myself when I realize that I am now considered to be a resource person for my community, and am called upon to share my experiences and ideas with others. This furthers my mission, and I am grateful that my website gives me the broader base from which to reach out to more people in need.

On the fun side, I've had some experiences that feel like they belong on a bucket list: being able to share my experience on television and radio shows. This allows me to grow even further, and I'm happy to do it, but I never forget my target audience--struggling moms who are trying to help their families live within their means and stay out of debt. I never forget where I started on this journey, or the hardships along the way.

By 2010, Mark and I were finally ready to think about moving from our small townhouse to another house better suited to our growing family.

We waited this long in order to pay our debt down even more, while at the same time saving for a healthy down payment. This is what we had learned from our disastrous house purchase in South Carolina, and we were now teaching about planning, budgeting, and living within one's means. We always intend to practice what we preach. In addition, I knew we were on a budget this time, but I wanted to find a house I loved, even if it was an older one. This time I wanted to fall in love with a house, and took the time to find one that suited our needs, had some character, and a good location for children.

The house that finally captured our hearts was a big 95-year-old two story Victorian home, close to town, near the library, and across the street from a park. It suited our new values in that it wasn't new or showy, but inviting, roomy and comfortable, with need for little TLC. And best of all, it was within our budget.

On the day we closed on our new "old" house, we found out that I was pregnant with our third child. Again, it felt like a sign. New beginnings. Our daughter was born in April, 2011. A Spring of blessings, for she came at a time when we had started getting really serious about paying down debt, and we had begun to gain some momentum on that front. But most importantly, our family was blessed yet again with a beautiful child.

BLOGS, BLOOPERS & BLUNDERS

Along the way in my determination to make the most of a deal, I tested the limits of store clerks, cashiers, managers, their computers, and yes, even my husband Mark. When I started to "Google" and explore the internet in South Carolina to learn about couponing, I was amazed at the deals I could find, and worked night and day figuring out ways to get the most out of them. It became my passion, or as some might say, my obsession. Mark was almost alarmed watching me, as I spent hours pouring over newspaper flyers, coupon websites, store policies, and anything to do with saving money. And I had to do this between my work at home and waitressing. But the more I dug into it, the more I discovered. And I was good at putting deals on top of deals, using store and manufacturer's coupons together on triple coupon days.

Some mornings in South Carolina, I would wake up at 5 a.m. to get to the grocery store during triple coupon sales. I would shop before Mark left for work, do half a dozen transactions that I had spent 15 hours putting together, and stocked up on groceries for the entire month for only $50! I would usually go with a friend and carpool, but one particular time we brought a new friend with us, who ended up getting sick in the parking lot. Instead of driving her home, we called her husband to come get her and continued shopping. That was not one of my prouder moments.

During the Christmas season of 2010, I decided to take advantage of the Black Friday sales. I was five months pregnant with our third child, and I stood in line at Toys R Us for two hours, from 8 until 10 p.m. to get the good deals when the doors opened at 10 a.m. I stayed out until 4 a.m. to get the best Black Friday deals for my kids because we were short on money, but wanted our children to have the best Christmas we could manage. This was the same year that I saved up $500, all the money for our Christmas, by completing consumer surveys that paid $3 - $5 apiece.

Needless to say, I was exhausted. It took me over a week to recover from that Toys R Us trip.

Mark supported my couponing, but after two years of every "date night" turning into a couponing trip, he finally told me that it was not allowed anymore. Week after week I would drag him to the grocery store, Walmart, Target, or anyplace to find a good deal. He never wanted to go when these times were supposed to be our special nights out, but I was almost addicted to couponing when I first started, and just had to find EVERY good deal. I still loved to shop (shades of the princess in our life before!), but this time I was addicted to saving money and getting deals. After driving my husband crazy off and on for five years, I was finally able to slow down and find balance. Getting every good deal is just not necessary, and honestly, it caused me to burn out. I am glad he put his foot down and told me "NO MORE"! I am thankful that I set a budget on my trips, because if I hadn't I would have easily gone over every week and gotten into more debt. I see this far too often with people I speak to, they coupon so much that they actually spend more money. Budgeting is so helpful in every area of your life!

While some of my early efforts at taking advantage of every deal were in fact, driving me and my family a little crazy, I got better and better at my planning. And more strategic. A more successful and very profitable shopping trip occurred about a year ago at my local Price Chopper and Lowe's. Mark and I needed new windows for our 95-year-old house, and this was going to be an expensive project, but we had finally saved up enough cash to buy them. I knew about using my grocery store purchases to get discounts on gas for our cars, and figured I would purchase gift cards at the grocery store to earn money for gas discounts.

I'd wrack up enough Price Chopper points to give me five free tanks of gas. Mark was my partner in this (it wasn't a date night!). I bought 87 Lowe's gift cards at the grocery store, and that weekend, he, always willing to go along with my rather unconventional schemes (now that he'd seen the results), took the grocery bag full of cards and drove off to Lowe's to turn them into the merchandise we needed. Given in increments of $20, $50, and $100, it was quite a pile of gift cards. Apparently, no one had done anything quite like this before, and the poor cashier who was presented with this was stunned. It took him several transactions to complete the sale. And the sheer number of transactions required to turn cards into windows, ultimately crashed the Lowe's computer. Oops! But Mark was his patient, unruffled self.

We got our windows, and they were installed shortly thereafter. Not only did we get new windows and with those, the bonus of lower heating bills, but for several months I was able to drive around by filling my tank up multiple times with FREE gas!

Looking over these "adventures," I can say that I learned a lot. And these sorts of experiences are among those I enjoy sharing with others on my blog. I still coupon, but in a more organized way, and I try to make it more fun for my kids, if they are along. My obsession was taking the joy out of my successes, and at times I lost sight of my children's (and husband's!) patience. But as a family, we're a team, and our children are very aware of our relationship with money. As Mark and I teach in our classes at church every week, the family has to be on the same page for financial fitness to work. In our house, even though my children are young, we're all in this together.

FINANCIAL FREEDOM

{Winter 2012}

After two years of living back home in New York, paying cash for everything, budgeting, and finding every way to save, Mark and I paid off our last student loan in January 2012. Except for our mortgage, we are now debt free. We still don't have credit cards--only two debit cards, one for each of us, and we now use cash for all groceries, gas, clothing, household items, furniture, and travel. And we'll never go back to our old ways, our old spending habits.

This entire journey out of debt caused us to rethink our value system, which now includes owing money to no one, and foregoing instant gratification for something much greater in the future.

Before all this, I never looked at prices, never knew how much was in our bank account, and as a result, paid recurring insufficient funds charges far too many times. Until we changed our mindset, Mark and I were a team in almost every way, but we didn't communicate much at all about money. We never sat down and discussed purchases, or made a budget.

Like many couples, we came into our relationship with different approaches to money. We didn't stop long enough to discuss or take advantage of our respective strengths in this area, but now we do. Mark is deliberate, calculating, and loves spreadsheets. I have a more intuitive sense of what we need as a family, from the day-to-day, nitty gritty details of managing the house, the food shopping and the kids' needs. Working together now, our combined skill sets have allowed us to maximize what we earn, and make sensible, meaningful decisions about our spending. We now communicate about money on a regular basis. And this is key: getting on the same page financially.

When we were first married and spending without care, we felt free and unrestricted. But the resulting debt load we accumulated was anything but freedom. It was a prison, taking away our time, energy, stability, and security. And we learned our lessons the hard way. Until we shredded our credit cards, it took us many attempts before we could stick with it, but we finally broke free of our old money habits. As Dr. Henry Cloud observed, "People's behavior changes when the pain of staying the same becomes greater than the pain of change."

Many people have asked me, now that I am "out of the woods," as it were, if my mindset could change yet again. Now that I know how to spend responsibly, would I consider getting a credit card and using it wisely? I can honestly answer, without any hesitation, "NO!" We regularly get credit card applications in the mail, some offering $300 in cash just to sign up. We've been tempted to sign on the line, get the reward, and cancel, but it is now a personal moral issue for us. We will never get another credit card.

I enjoy my new life, and the challenge of living frugally. I still go hunting at garage sales on weekends with my kids, each with their own hard-earned money in hand to spend. I know that they are learning by the examples we set. Most of our furniture is second hand, from Craig's List or garage sales. And I am content.

Best of all, Mark and I know what we value, what we want out of life. And it can't be bought. We have four healthy, beautiful children, a roof over our heads, and the love and respect of one another in a strong marriage. This is what financial freedom looks like to us.

I will never go back to the nightmare of crushing debt, fear of checking the mailbox, paying off one credit card with another, or transferring to 0% credit cards with the false sense of saving money. I no longer buy impulsively, without regard for the consequences to my family's budget and our future. With four children under the age of nine, a new goal is saving for college. This is a value, and we now put our money where our values are. Or, to put it another way, our spending is now a reflection of our values.

We love to be together as a family, so we save for vacations, and go as often as money and time allow. We tithe to our church. Through my friend's organization, we started giving aid to an orphanage in Rwanda, and contribute to a publication for the homeless in our former home city, Charlotte. We now have the financial means to do these things, and are able to give more as we have more resources available to us.

But it's not just money that we give. Another new value, shared by both Mark and me, is our growing desire to teach others how to achieve financial fitness-to avoid the pitfalls of our mistakes, or, if they're already in crisis, to help them work their way out. I think we made about every mistake that could be made, and yet we ultimately succeeded. If we can do it, so can you. That is our constant message. I continue to give talks about living frugally, and counsel individuals who are in need of financial guidance. Once a week at our church, Mark and I have offered classes to help those who want to learn from our lessons in saving money and spending wisely. We're not professionals; we're a married couple who got into horrible debt, and worked our way out over a several years. Our lessons were learned from experience, so our classes are honest, practical, and from the heart. We get to work together as a team again, but this time as teachers and counselors. It's time we spend together, and time we enjoy.

Recently, with the joyful discovery of my fourth pregnancy, Mark and I discussed buying a new house. Bigger, to better accommodate our growing family, and with a few more conveniences than our older, more modest home affords us.

We went so far as to contact a realtor, find what we thought was our new dream house, and sign on the dotted line. But then, something stopped us. I was juggling too much-- five months pregnant, trying to keep my website going, and supporting Mark in his career. All the while, I was also doing all the things that a stay-at-home-mom does— WE finally had the income to send our daughters to dance classes, doctor appointments, play groups, and keeping up with housework and laundry.

Suddenly this decision didn't feel good. Mark and I both sensed it. So rather than the rash "jump" that we took in South Carolina in that summer of 2006, we sat down and talked about it. Was this really a value? Could we make our modest home work with a fourth child? And with some creative planning, we began to reconfigure space and possibilities. Again, as I so often did in times of doubt, I prayed, asking God for guidance.

In the end, we decided against buying the house. Both Mark and I felt a great sense of relief in this decision. We were able to focus more on our children, our work, and our newfound freedom in a life without debt.

SILVER LININGS

Soon afterwards, I realized how far we'd come in our journey. We opted out of the contract, and moved my office into our bedroom to make a nursery for the baby. And the silver lining--I redecorated our bedroom, something I'd planned to do for a while, but was always putting off. So now a room that was once a bit shabby, is now a lovely sanctuary for both Mark and me.

My office is now in the corner--just a desk and my computer, and at night, Mark slips in and reads on the bed. The entire room is newly made over with some items I got at Lowe's, Big Lots, garage sales, and some things in my basement. The paint on the walls is my favorite color, a soft teal, and the canopy over our old queen bed makes the room look contemporary, new, and inviting-- a place where Mark likes to just sit quietly and read while I'm tapping away at my desk. And I remade this little haven for us for under $100. Certainly less than the cost of a new, bigger, and "better" house.

MY LEGACY

Looking back over the past 11 years, I am still amazed at my journey. At 23 I was a director level sales professional in a business suit. Now, at 33, I am a stay-at-home-mom in sweats, still working, but out of my house, with an occasional trip to give talks, counsel women, and share my story with others.

I remember those three years in South Carolina, of never eating out, never spending an extra dime, and the year in our little townhouse in New York, where we didn't have enough stuff to hold a garage sale if we'd wanted one. I know the sacrifices that Mark, my children, and me made. We will never go back to living beyond our means. We are no longer tempted by the stuff paraded across the T.V. and internet day and night, or the things we bought recklessly, in our early years as newlyweds. We are now wiser, but fortunately for us, not a lot older!

Do we eat out now? Yes, and sometimes at nice restaurants, but with cash.

Do we occasionally buy special things? Yes. Mark recently bought me a beautiful Michael Kors bag for my business trips-- I felt it was extravagant at first, but now I realize it was his way of telling me that he was proud of my success. When I traveled to New York City to appear on WNBC's Valentine's Day Special, to share ideas about having a frugal holiday, that bag reminded me somehow that I had "made it," that I had conquered my fears and forged ahead to make a new and better life, by hard work, my wits, and with the support of my amazing husband. No one had to know that I was wearing a ($100) Max Studio designer dress that I'd purchased at an online thrift shop for $10 *(how to save money on clothing).

And despite the hardships of the South Carolina years, I am grateful that I learned the couponing skills there, and was able to bring them to women in my new hometown in Upstate New York, where there were few resources of that kind. Through my website, I've been able to give back to my community, and that is a key value in my life. I want to fulfill the promise I made to God, not to waste the gifts he gave me. Helping others is my passion, my calling, and through my church, my website, and now, this book, I hope to continue to help others to learn to live more financially fit lives.

Most importantly, I know, from little daily occurrences, that my new way of living is being passed on to my children. A few months ago, my son and I went out "hunting" at a local garage sale--something we enjoy doing together.*{Insert garage sale video link} He was going to take $9, the total of his savings.

I suggested that he might want to save a little rather than bringing all his money. He reconsidered, and decided to bring $4. At the sale, he found a Transformer figure he'd been looking for priced at $2. I felt it was overpriced (yes, I know my price points at garage sales!), so I suggested he approach the woman hosting the garage sale, and ask if she might come down in her price. He took my suggestion, she agreed to $1, and he came back triumphant, with his action figure in one hand and a dollar in the other. He'd learned to buy smarter by negotiating, and walked away with both his toy and money left over.

On another occasion, my son and I

were shopping at one of our favorite bargain stores, T.J. Maxx, and he found a toy he'd been looking for--The Sonic Hedgehog Racecar. The problem was, it was one dollar more than he had. He asked me if he could borrow the money from me, but I said no. Instead, I offered to take him home and earn that dollar by doing a couple of household chores. I also promised him that we would return that day to the store for the racecar. He agreed, and when we got home, he energetically cleaned up his bedroom and the backyard.

I gave him his earned dollar, and saw the sense of accomplishment on his face. True to my word, we drove right back to the store, where he bought the toy with his own money. Lesson learned. And then some. I did not just give him the dollar, which would have been easy, and eliminated the extra trip back home and then again to the store, but I taught him a valuable lesson. And I knew then that not only was I a more responsible person financially, but a better parent.

Most recently, Mark told me about an exchange he had with our eight-year-old son that warmed my heart. He was in the kitchen doing dishes, while our son was in the other room watching T.V. He came running into the kitchen to tell his dad to "quick, come into the living room" to see this great deal on T.V.

He was excited as he told his father, "Dad, you've got to try this! You save pennies a day and in the end you get $100,000!" What our son didn't realize was that he was watching an ad for Gerber Baby Grow Up Life Insurance, and that to get that money someone would have to die! That was not mentioned in the commercial. When Mark explained this to our son, he looked surprised, a little disappointed, and then walked out of the room. It wasn't quite the "lottery win" that it sounded like.

But the fact that our son wanted to share that with his dad showed us that even at a young age, he is aware of our feelings about money, and wants to help contribute--even if it's finding good deals on T.V. It made us realize just how much our mindset has influenced our family. If this is my legacy, then I am truly successful.

MY NEWLY FOUND PASSION

I love God, I love my family--my wonderful husband Mark, and our four children. But I know as a woman, wife, mother, and entrepreneur, that it's important in my life, to carve out time and energy for me. So what makes me tick?

I love romantic (and quiet!) dinners out with Mark, trips with my family, my volunteer work at church, and helping those in need--both close to home and far away. I am grateful for the platform that my website has given me to reach out to other women in debt, who feel hopeless, out of control, and unsure where to turn. Sharing the story of my mistakes and blunders along the road to my financial stability is important to me, because it keeps things real and "relatable." After all, I am always one step away from repeating this pattern.

But I also love fun and silly things. I cruise through Pinterest and Facebook daily, to check on friends and share interests about decorating my house or coming up with activities for my kids. I love quiet time alone to read and think, lunches with friends, time with my parents and extended family, cuddling with my children, and of course, spending time with Mark. And once I lost the weight of my financial mess, I was free to pursue my real interests and the things I truly love.

My philosophy in a nutshell is this: make your spending a reflection of your values. If your life has spun out of control financially, it may be time to take a look at where your money is going and why. Since I've gone through this I can share some things from my toolbox--things I've learned through experience that really work, and that won't overwhelm an already stressed-out mom. Small, simple things that can be done, even with a kitchen sink full of dirty dishes and bedrooms full of unmade beds.

I'm definitely not preaching perfection. That, by definition, is unattainable. We all have our weaknesses when it comes to spending (mine is purses!), but while you're getting back on track, you'll probably have to give up some of your once considered "must haves." That does not necessarily mean forever, for once you have achieved financial stability you may have the means to buy those things again,(and buy them smarter) or you may decide you don't even want them. They are not in your value system. They may no longer seem so important or necessary.

So join me on this journey to discover your own talents, strengths, and creativity. Put those skills into action, and maybe you will be able to begin moving in a direction that you want to go -- toward a sense of control over your life.

The work is simple but not easy. And the rewards? They will be different for each of you, but I can guarantee that you will feel a great sense of accomplishment if you start on this journey to regain control of your spending and your life.

One of my greatest rewards is my 2004 green minivan, or what I like to call my Badge of Honor. Cars played a large part in our financial struggle. Mark had been a "car guy," and we bought and sold many cars over our long journey. From his first $500 "rustbucket," to the Audi and my luxury company car lease, we ran the gamut of "wheels." And car loans. They represented some of the poor choices we made-- impulsive, not thoughtful, and not reflecting our value system.

In November 2007, we needed a second vehicle, after living as a one-car family for eight months. We finally sat down and discussed the best options--something reasonably priced, reliable, and not too expensive to repair, and most likely, used. We had hoped to have a big family, even though at the time I was having fertility problems, so we decided on a minivan. With the help of a friend who had access to an auto auction, we were able to get the used van we'd hoped for, and closed the deal. We put a lot of thought into this purchase, and it has turned out to be everything I'd hoped for. It's now nine years old, has about 130,000 miles on the odometer, and runs like a champ. It's reliable, has never needed a major repair, and I love it. It's not fancy, carries no status; it's just practical.

But it represents so much to me--the shift in my mindset, our new joint planning of major purchases, and living within our means. Even though we could now replace it with a newer, fancier version, I don't want to. I'll drive it until the wheels fall off. Every time my family, all six of us, buckle in and take off for church, the park, the grocery store or soccer practice, I know we've done well.

It was worth it

With true financial freedom comes the ability to do something that at one time seemed impossible. This is what happened in December of 2013. As I was finishing up this book, we decided to make this HUGE decision and a correspondingly huge risk. The past few years I kept on asking the question "Is this it? When are we going to start living life?" We had worked so hard to be financially free, yet felt like we were stuck in park.

Mark has always worked long hours and had a long commute to work, out the door at 6:30 am, and back at 6:00 pm. Our children go to bed at 7 pm, so that gives him around 30 minutes after dinnertime to hang out with our children. I really miss my husband when he is gone; we are one of those couples that really enjoys spending time together. I get lonely during the day, the kids miss him, and we feel like we cannot do anything but work, take care of the kids, and then collapse from exhaustion at night. After we had our fourth baby and she became colicky, we began to re-prioritize our life. Did we really want to let this life pass us by? The answer was no, and we had an option that not many have.

The hard work, diligence, and sacrifice we made over the past six years is now allowing us to have a freedom that we never dreamt possible; Mark and I are able to stay home together, work together on our websites iamthatlady.com and MarkandLaurenG.com. We can raise our children together, and enjoy this life.

It might be easy to think of budgeting as a restriction. And in the short-term, it is. But long-term, it is incredibly freeing. The financial freedom we have now has far exceeded anything those credit cards could have ever offered us. It took years of sacrifice on our part. I remember when we had to move the table during dinner to get the milk out. The times of having to forgo that $1.00 cup of coffee. And I think to myself – "Yes, it was worth it." Every single sacrifice we made was worth it.

Made in the USA
San Bernardino, CA
29 November 2016